The story of Easter

A book of 30 Bible readings and notes
to help you worship and pray

Derek Thompson and Suzy Edmundson

Edited by Tony Phelps-Jones

Published by Scripture Union, 207–209 Queensway, Bletchley, MK2 2EB, England
Email: info@scriptureunion.org.uk
Internet: www.scriptureunion.org.uk

© Copyright all editions Causeway PROSPECTS
First published in 2006
ISBN 1 84427 217 6

Causeway PROSPECTS is a division of PROSPECTS for People with Learning Disabilities and their address is PO Box 351, Reading, RG30 4XQ. Phone 0118 9516 978. Email causeway@prospects.org.uk

About Causeway Prospects: Causeway PROSPECTS provides resource materials and training to equip churches for effective outreach and ministry among people with learning disabilities. It also runs holiday weekends and special ministry at Spring Harvest and the Keswick Convention.

British Library Cataloguing-in-Publication Data: a catalogue record for this book is available from the British Library.

Scripture portions are taken from The Holy Bible: English Version for the Deaf (published as the Easy-to-Read Version) © 2000 by the World Bible Translation Center, Inc. and used with permission. Internet: www.wbtc.com

Icons © Widgit Software Ltd 2002, developed by the Rebus Symbol Development Project, designed by Cate Detheridge and used with kind permission.

Cover design by David Lund Design: www.davidlund-design.com

Internal page layout by Creative Pages: www.creativepages.org.uk

Printed and bound in Great Britain by goodmanbaylis, The Trinity Press, Worcester, UK.

Scripture Union is an international charity working with churches in more than 130 countries providing resources to bring the good news about Jesus Christ to children, young people and families – and to encourage them to develop spiritually through the Bible and prayer. As well as a network of volunteers, staff and associates who run holidays, church-based events and school Christian groups, we produce a wide range of publications and support those who use our resources through training programmes.

Using this book

 The story of Easter and the other titles in this series are intended to help you to worship and pray. On each page there is a reading from the Bible, some thoughts and a prayer.

 The readings are from the *Easy-to-Read Version* (ETRV), a very clear and simple translation of the Bible. The reading printed each day is quite short. A longer reading is also given if you would like to read more using your own Bible. There is a list of key words and their meanings near the back of the book.

Reading the Bible

The Bible, which is sometimes called the Word of God, is not really one book but a whole library of many books. The 66 books were written by many people who God spoke to at different times. At the front of the Bible you will find a list of the titles of all the books in the Bible and the page number where each book begins.

To help you find your way around such a big book, little groups of one or two sentences have been numbered, and then groups of those sentences have been collected into chapters.

So how do you find the one or two sentences that you want in the Bible? Let's say you want to find Matthew 5:5,6. That means you need to look in the book called Matthew, in chapter number 5 and verses 5 and 6.

You can find Matthew in the list of books at the front of the Bible. This tells you which page Matthew starts on. When

3

you have turned to the beginning of Matthew you then search for chapter 5. Look down the page until you see the numbers 5 and 6. Those are the sentences (or verses) that you need.

When you do your Bible reading, try to spend a few extra minutes praying and worshipping. Praying is talking and listening to God. You can do this aloud or without using words. You can pray on your own or with friends. Worship is telling God how much you love him, through words or songs, or things you do. This can be singing in church, but it's a lot more than that. It's about enjoying the wonderful world God has made. It's about how we speak to each other. It's about how we live our lives.

As you pray you can:

 thank God for his goodness and his help;

 tell God how great he is, and that you love him;

 ask God to help you, your friends, your family and other people.

If you are a helper using this book with someone who does not read, you will find guidance notes at the end.

The *Easy-to-Read Version* of the Bible is available to buy from Causeway PROSPECTS.

The story of Easter

1 God's wonderful love

 Yes, God loved the world so much that he gave his only Son. God gave his Son so that every person that believes in him would not be lost, but have life forever. John 3:16 (Full reading John 3:16,17)

 When God made people like us, everything was good. But then people spoiled it all. They started to fight. They spoiled God's world. And that made God very sad.

But God loved the people he had made, and God loves you and me. God wants to take us into his special, loving family for ever.

So God sent his only son, Jesus, to put things right. In this book, we'll find out what Jesus did, and what happened that very first Easter.

 Father God, thank you for loving us. Help me to understand what Jesus did that first Easter. Amen.

2 Jesus knows what it's like

Then the Spirit [God] sent Jesus into the desert alone. Jesus was in the desert 40 days ... While Jesus was in the desert, he was tempted by Satan (the devil).
Mark 1:12,13 (Full reading Mark 1:12,13)

All of us want to do things we shouldn't sometimes, even when we know they're wrong.

God wanted Jesus to know what it is like for us. So God let the devil try to make Jesus do something wrong. The devil tempted Jesus. The devil hates God. So the devil tried to stop Jesus from showing people how much God loves them.

The devil wants us to do bad things. But we don't need to be afraid. Whenever we feel like doing bad things, Jesus will help us not to.

Lord Jesus, help me to pray to you when I want to do something wrong. Send your Spirit to help me to do the right things instead. Amen.

3 What's really important

Jesus ate nothing for 40 days and nights. After this, he was very hungry... The devil said, 'If you are the Son of God, tell these rocks to become bread.' Jesus answered him, 'It is written in the Scriptures [Bible], "It is not just bread that keeps people alive. People's lives depend on what God says".' Matthew 4:2–4 (Full reading Matthew 4:1–4)

Jesus was very hungry in the desert. But Jesus stayed there because it was a good place for him to think about God.

The devil tried to make Jesus think about food instead of thinking about God.

Jesus could easily have changed rocks (stones) into bread. Instead, Jesus told the devil that finding out what God wants is more important than food.

Ask God to help you to think of something you really like to eat, or something you especially like to do. If you want, you can give up that thing for a time. Ask God to help you. Then you will know how Jesus felt.

4 Don't show off!

The devil put Jesus on a very high place of the temple. He [the devil] said to Jesus, 'If you are the Son of God, jump off!' ... Jesus answered, '... it also says in the Scriptures [Bible]: "You must not test (doubt) the Lord your God".'
Luke 4:9–12 (Full reading Luke 4:9–12)

Jesus did lots of wonderful things. Jesus could easily have jumped off a high building like the temple. God would have kept him safe. Then people would have thought Jesus was like Superman!

But Jesus knew God didn't want him to show off. God had sent Jesus to do things the way God wanted. So Jesus told the devil what the Bible said.

We need to do things the way God wants. It doesn't matter what people think.

Father God, help me not to do things just to show off in front of people. Show me what you want me to do instead. Amen.

5 Jesus the teacher

**Jesus went everywhere in the country ...
Jesus taught in the synagogues (churches)
and told the Good News about the kingdom
of heaven. And Jesus healed all the people's
diseases and sicknesses. The news about
Jesus spread.**
Matthew 4:23,24 (Full reading Matthew 4:23–25)

You can read in the Bible about all the wonderful
things Jesus did. Jesus taught people how God
wanted them to live. Jesus helped people to get
well. And Jesus told people how one day they
could be with God for ever. It must have been
wonderful to meet Jesus like those people did.

We can learn everything we need to know about
Jesus from the Bible. Pray for the minister or
group leader who helps you to understand the
Bible.

**Father God, thank you for Jesus. And thank
you for the people (say their names) who
teach me about Jesus. Help me to be a good
learner. Amen.**

Then Jesus talked to the twelve apostles [his helpers] alone. Jesus said to them, 'Listen! We are going to Jerusalem. Everything that God told the prophets to write about the Son of Man [Jesus] will happen! His people will turn against him and give him to the non-Jewish people. The non-Jews will laugh at him, insult him, and spit on him ... beat him with whips and then kill him! But on the third day after his death, he will rise to life again.'

Luke 18:31–33 (Full reading Luke 18:31–34)

It was time for Jesus to do the most important thing God wanted. In Jerusalem people would treat him badly and then kill him. But then God would bring Jesus back to life again!

God had already told special men called prophets all about it, hundreds of years before. God meant it all to happen like it did.

Dear God, thank you for keeping your promises. Help me always to keep the promises I make. Amen.

7 Welcome the king!

**Jesus was coming close to Jerusalem ...
[Jesus' friends and helpers] were very
excited and praised God ... They said,
'Welcome! God bless the king that comes in
the name of the Lord! Peace in heaven and
glory to God!'**
Luke 19:37,38 (Full reading Luke 19:37,38)

So Jesus went to Jerusalem. When Jesus got
there, he wasn't riding in a beautiful carriage with
horses, like an important man. Jesus came on a
little donkey. Jesus didn't care about looking
important. Jesus cared about the ordinary people
all around him. Crowds of people were there to
meet him. These people knew that Jesus had
come from God.

**Father God, thank you for all those people
who welcomed Jesus. They didn't know
what he had come to do. They were just so
excited to see him. Help me to be excited
too when I think about Jesus. Amen.**

8 At the temple

 Jesus went into the temple area. He began to throw out the people that were selling things there. Jesus said, 'It is written in the Scriptures [Bible], "My house will be a house of prayer". But you have changed it into a "hiding place for thieves".'
Luke 19:45,46 (Full reading Luke 19:45,46)

 The temple was like a church. It was a very special place where people went to worship God. The people used to buy offerings (like presents) to give to God. But the people in charge of the temple shops were cheats. They used to make the people pay too much money for the presents they bought.

Jesus was angry because God's special temple was being spoiled.

 Father God, help me to understand how angry it makes you when people do bad things and cheat and hurt others. I pray for the church I go to, that people feel safe and loved when they come. Amen.

14

9 Wanting to kill Jesus

Jesus taught the people in the temple area every day. The leading priests, the teachers of the law, and some of the leaders of the people wanted to kill Jesus.
Luke 19:47,48 (Full reading Luke 19:47,48)

Many of the temple priests didn't believe in Jesus. They didn't think Jesus was God's son.

Because the priests were in charge of the temple, the priests felt very important. But now huge crowds of people were coming to listen to Jesus. The priests were afraid the people would think Jesus was more important than the priests. The priests were afraid of what might happen next.

It is sometimes hard for church leaders to know what is the best thing to do.

Lord Jesus, I pray for church leaders (say their names) to know what are the right things to do each day, and not to be afraid about what will happen. Amen.

10 Judas

 One of Jesus' twelve apostles was named Judas Iscariot. Satan (the devil) went into Judas and made him do a bad thing. Judas went and talked with the leading priests and some of the soldiers ... they promised to give Judas money if he would give Jesus to them.
Luke 22:3–5 (Full reading Luke 22:3–6)

 Do you remember how the devil tried to stop Jesus doing what God wanted? Now the devil spoke to Judas. Judas listened to the devil.

Judas was a thief. He used to steal some of the money that people gave Jesus and his friends to buy food. Judas thought he could get more money if he told the priests where they could find Jesus and take him prisoner.

 Father God, help me never to want money so much that I would do bad things to get it. Help me to remember that you will give me what I need. Amen.

16

11 The Last Supper

 The time came for them to eat the Passover meal. Jesus and the apostles [his friends] were together at the table. Jesus said to them, 'I wanted very much to eat this Passover meal with you before I die.'
Luke 22:14,15 (Full reading Luke 22:14–16)

 The Passover meal was a special meal. Every year when people ate the Passover meal, they remembered all the wonderful things God had done for them. This Passover meal was different. Jesus knew it was his last meal. Soon, Judas would go out to tell the priests where he was. And then, the priests and the soldiers would come to take Jesus away.

It must have been a sad time, but it was a very special one. We call this meal the Last Supper.

 Think back to a special time when you had a meal with friends. In your prayers today thank God for those friends and pray for them.

12 This bread is my body

Then Jesus took some bread. He thanked God for the bread and divided it. He gave it to the apostles [his friends]. Then Jesus said, 'This bread is my body that I am giving for you. Eat this to remember me.'
Luke 22:19 (Full reading Luke 22:19)

Jesus knew the soldiers would soon take him away and kill him. Jesus was going to die so all the people who believe in him can be forgiven. Jesus wanted his friends to remember. So Jesus asked each of them to eat a piece of bread, and think what was going to happen to Jesus' body.

Nowadays in church we still do that. We eat a piece of bread and drink a sip of wine or juice to remember what Jesus has done for us. We call that Holy Communion or the Lord's Supper.

Think about Jesus on that night. Then say thank you to Jesus for dying for you and for everyone. Amen.

13 God's new promise

**In the same way, after supper, Jesus took
the cup of wine and said, 'This wine shows
the new agreement from God to his people.
This new agreement begins with my blood
(death) that I am giving for you.'**
Luke 22:20 (Full reading Luke 22:12–19)

After giving his friends the bread, Jesus asked
them to take a sip of wine and to think of Jesus'
blood. When Jesus was on the cross a soldier
stabbed him with a sharp spear, and Jesus' blood
poured out. The wine Jesus gave them was red,
like blood.

Because of what Jesus has done, anyone who
believes in him can be forgiven for every bad thing,
and belong to God's family for ever.

**As you pray today, think of God's promise
that if you believe in Jesus and you have
asked God to forgive you, then you are part
of God's family. Tell God how you feel about
that and thank him for Jesus.**

14 Love each other

 I give you a new command: Love each other. You must love each other like I loved you.
John 13:34 (Full reading John 13:34,35)

 Jesus doesn't want us just to like people. Jesus wants us to love people. Jesus wants us to do things for people even if it's hard.

When it's hard to love people, we can always pray to Jesus. Jesus will help us to love them.

You already know some of the things you are good at doing for people. It might be giving a smile, or sending a get well card if they are sick, or doing little jobs for them if they are tired. Think of the things you know how to do.

 Lord Jesus, thank you for the things I can do. Help me to do those things well. Help me to ask you if I don't know what to do. Amen.

15 Promising the Holy Spirit

 I will ask the Father, and he will give you another Helper. He will give you this Helper to be with you forever.
John 14:16 (Full reading John 14:15–17)

 Jesus knows that sometimes it's hard to do things for him. So Jesus promised us a helper. The helper is the Holy Spirit.

We can't see the Holy Spirit but he's always there and he helps us to think and pray and understand what we read in the Bible.

The Holy Spirit is a special friend we can always rely on. He knows how we feel. He knows what we are thinking. He helps us to do what is right. He shows us how to do the loving things we are good at.

 Father God, thank you for the Holy Spirit, my special helper. Thank you for always being with me, so I am never alone. Amen.

16 Jesus gives peace

 I leave you peace. It is my own peace I give you.
John 14:27 (Full reading John 14:27)

 Jesus knew that he was going to die. He knew that his friends would be afraid and wonder what was going to happen to them.

Jesus knew that people would be mean to his friends, too. So Jesus wanted his friends to have a special kind of peace.

When we know what God is like, we know God will never leave us. God will never let us down. God will forgive us when we get things wrong. We can feel calm and still and safe, whatever happens to us. That's the sort of peace Jesus wants all of us to have.

 Lord Jesus, when I'm afraid or lonely, help me to remember the peace you give me. Help me to know I am safe with God for ever. Amen.

17 Doing what God says

I will not talk with you much longer ... But the world must know that I love the Father. So I do exactly what the Father told me to do.
John 14:30,31 (Full reading John 14:30,31)

Jesus was going to do exactly what his father God wanted. Jesus wanted the whole world to know. So, after Jesus died, his friends went round telling people what he had done. Then the Bible was written, so people like us can read about Jesus.

Soon the whole world will know, just like Jesus wanted.

You can tell people about Jesus too. If it's hard for you to talk, don't worry. Just do kind things for people, like Jesus did. That will help people understand what Jesus is like.

Father God, thank you for Jesus who showed everyone how he loved you. Help me to tell people about Jesus. Help me to show people what your love is like by everything I do. Amen.

18 Jesus prays to his father

 Jesus left the city (Jerusalem) and went to the Mount of Olives ... (Jesus went there often.) Luke 22:39,40 (Full reading Luke 22:39–44).

 Jesus' favourite place was a garden called Gethsemane. It was a lovely, quiet place. There Jesus prayed to God. Jesus was going to do what God wanted, but Jesus knew how painful it was going to be. So Jesus told God just how he felt, and God sent angels to be with him and make him strong.

Whatever God wants us to do, he will always be there for us to pray to. There is nothing we dare not tell God. God understands. God will make us strong too.

 Think of the things that make you afraid. Talk to God about them, just quietly on your own. Then God will make you strong, like he made Jesus strong.

19 A kiss from Judas

While Jesus was still speaking, Judas came there ... Judas had many people with him ... Judas planned to do something to show the people which man was Jesus. Judas said, 'The man I kiss is Jesus. Arrest him and guard him while you lead him away.'
Mark 14:43,44 (Full reading Mark 14:43–45)

Judas went up to Jesus, and kissed Jesus on the cheek. Then the men grabbed Jesus and took him away. Next day, Judas was sorry. He tried to give back the money he got for giving up Jesus. The priests wouldn't take the money back. So Judas threw the money away, and hanged himself.

If we have done something bad, we need to say sorry to God. If we do, God says he will forgive us. We may need to say sorry to the person we've hurt as well.

Dear God, I am sorry for any bad things I've done. (Think about them for a minute). Please forgive me. Amen.

20 Jesus on trial

The leading priests and all the Jewish council tried to find something that Jesus had done wrong so they could kill him ... Many people came and told false things against Jesus. But the people all said different things – none of them agreed.
Mark 14:55,56 (Full reading Mark 14:53–56)

The Jewish council (the leaders of the Jewish people) and the priests wanted to have Jesus killed. But they wanted to look as if they were in the right. So they got lots of people to tell lies about Jesus. But they couldn't prove that Jesus had done anything wrong.

If people tell us things we don't think are true, we can pray to God about it. Then we will know if those people are telling us lies.

Father God, thank you for all the good people who run our country and teach in our churches. Help them to do everything really well and always tell the truth. Amen.

21 Telling the truth

The high priest asked Jesus another question: 'Are you the Christ, the Son of the blessed God? Jesus answered, 'Yes, I am the Son of God.' ... All the people said that Jesus was wrong. They said he was guilty and must be killed.
Mark 14:61–64 (Full reading Mark 14:61–64)

Then the high priest asked Jesus if he was the Son of God. Jesus said he was. Jesus was telling the truth, but the high priest wouldn't believe it. So the high priest told the people that when Jesus said he was God's son, Jesus was telling lies. The people got very angry, and said Jesus must be killed. Some of the people spat on Jesus and punched him.

Jesus always told the truth.

Father God, help me tell the truth like Jesus did that night, even if people are shouting and saying I'm wrong. Help me never to tell lies, even if I am afraid. Amen.

22 Stop the bullying!

Herod asked Jesus many questions, but Jesus said nothing ... Then Herod and his soldiers laughed at Jesus. They made fun of Jesus by dressing him in clothes like kings wear.
Luke 23:9–11 (Full reading Luke 23:8–11)

King Herod was a cruel man and he didn't care about Jesus. Jesus wouldn't speak to him. So King Herod made fun of Jesus.

King Herod was a bully. He thought it was funny to dress Jesus up in a king's clothes, and laugh at him. But King Herod didn't know the truth. Jesus really is a king, the greatest king of all.

Do people bully anyone you know? If people make fun of someone or push them about or make them do things they don't want to, that's bullying. And it's bad.

Dear God, I pray for anyone who is being bullied or treated badly. Please show me if there is anything I can do to stop it. Amen.

23 Love from the cross

Jesus and the two criminals were led to a place called 'The Skull'. There the soldiers nailed Jesus to his cross ... Jesus said, 'Father, forgive these people that are killing me. They don't know what they are doing.' Luke 23:33,34 (Full reading Luke 23:32–34)

The soldiers nailed Jesus through his hands and feet to a big wooden cross, and sat down to wait for him to die. This was what soldiers did to punish people.

The soldiers were cruel men. But the soldiers were just doing what they were told.   As Jesus waited to die, he thought about those soldiers and asked his father God to forgive them.

The Bible says the soldiers just laughed at him. But nothing stopped Jesus from loving them, just like Jesus loves you and me.

Father God, help me to love people, even when they are mean or laugh at me. Amen.

24 Jesus dies

At noon the whole country became dark. This darkness continued until three o'clock. At three o'clock Jesus cried with a loud voice ... 'My God, my God, why have you left me alone?' ... Then Jesus cried with a loud voice, and died.
Mark 15:33,34,37 (Full reading Mark 15:33–39)

This is a sad and horrible story to read. But God wants us to understand it.

When people do wrong things, it is like they are shut away from God. When Jesus died, he took the blame for all the wrong things everyone has ever done so that nobody would ever have to be shut away from God again.

When Jesus died, he got shut away from God, instead of us.

If you believe in Jesus, thank him quietly for what he did for you. If you're not sure about Jesus, don't be afraid. God will forgive you, if you ask him to. It's like God is holding out his arms to you.

25 Why did Jesus die?

Christ [Jesus] himself died for you. And that one death paid for your sins. He [Jesus] was not guilty, but he died for people who are guilty. He did this to bring you all to God.
1 Peter 3:18 (Full reading 1 Peter 3:18)

Jesus had done nothing wrong. Jesus knew that God is always angry about the wrong things people do.

So Jesus let himself be punished for those wrong things and for the wrong things we do too. Because of Jesus we can be forgiven and join God's family.

As you pray today's prayer, think what it means to be in God's family. God is your father and Jesus is your brother.

Father God, thank you for all that Jesus has done for me. Please forgive me for all the things I have done that hurt you. Please send your Spirit to make me part of your family. Amen.

26 Jesus is buried

Later, a man named Joseph ... asked ... for the body of Jesus ... Nicodemus went with Joseph ... These two men took Jesus' body ... In the garden there was a new tomb [grave] ... The men put Jesus in that tomb ...
John 19:38–42 (Full reading John 19:38–42)

Jesus was buried by two of his friends. One friend was called Nicodemus. Nicodemus put special perfume on Jesus' body.

The other friend was called Joseph. Joseph was very rich. He was a good man and he believed in Jesus. Joseph carefully wrapped Jesus' body in a clean cloth. They laid Jesus in a tomb, like a cave in the rock.

Joseph and Nicodemus must have been very sad. They were afraid. But they wanted to do these last things for Jesus.

Father God, thank you for those good, kind men who buried Jesus. Help me to be brave and do good things for you even when I am afraid. Amen.

27 He's alive!

Very early Sunday morning, the women came to the tomb (grave) where Jesus' body was laid ... A heavy stone had been put in the doorway to close the tomb. But the women found that the stone was rolled away. They went in, but they did not find the Lord Jesus' body.
Luke 24:1–3 (Full reading Luke 24:1–8)

The women followers loved Jesus very much. They went to look after his dead body. But the body was gone.

Two angels in shining clothes said to the women, 'Jesus is not here. He has risen from death!' Suddenly, the women remembered what Jesus had said. Jesus had told them he would be killed, but then, on the third day, he would rise from the dead!

Every Easter Sunday in church we show how happy we are that Jesus is alive. Sometimes it's almost like a party!

Say thank you to God for bringing Jesus back from the dead. God is powerful. He can do anything!

28 Jesus visits his friends

The day was Sunday. That same evening the followers (Jesus' friends) were together. The doors were locked, because they were afraid ... Then Jesus came and stood among them ... John 20:19 (Full reading John 20:19,20)

When Jesus had been taken away by the soldiers, most of his friends ran away. Now they were all hiding in a locked room. They were afraid the Jews and the soldiers would come to get them too. They didn't dare go back home. They didn't know what to do.

Then suddenly Jesus came in. The locked door didn't stop him. Jesus said, 'Peace be with you!'

Jesus' friends were so happy! From that time on, they weren't afraid any more.

Lord Jesus, thank you for dying for me and coming back to life again. When I am afraid, help me to know that you are with me, and that you love me. Amen.

29 Doubting Thomas

Then Jesus said to Thomas, 'Put your finger here. Look at my hands. Put your hand here in my side. Stop doubting and start believing.'
John 20:27 (Full reading John 20:24–29).

When Jesus came to his friends, one of them called Thomas wasn't there. So the others told Thomas what had happened. But Thomas couldn't believe Jesus was alive again until he had seen Jesus for himself.

So Jesus came back a second time, just for Thomas. Then Thomas believed.

Thomas called Jesus his Lord and his God. Thomas wanted to do everything Jesus said.

Do you know someone who isn't sure that Jesus is really alive? Jesus will be patient with them, too. Ask Jesus to help you when you tell people about him.

Dear Lord Jesus, please help me when I talk about you so that I can help people to understand. Amen.

30 You can have life

 ... these things are written so that you can believe that Jesus is the Christ, the Son of God. Then, by believing, you can have life through his name.
John 20:31 (Full reading John 20:30,31)

 If we believe in Jesus, we will be part of God's family for ever. Not just here on earth but in heaven too.

Jesus died for us at Easter. Then Jesus came back from the dead, because nothing can kill him. One day, every one of us will die. Then, if we believe in Jesus, it will be just like we wake up again and we will be with Jesus in heaven for ever. It will be more wonderful than we can imagine. Hallelujah! Praise the Lord!

 Dear God, thank you for the promise of heaven. Help me to put you first in my life every day and to share your love with others. Amen.

Key words

Angels   Special servants of God who bring messages from him or help us.

Apostles   People chosen by Jesus to be his special helpers.

Criminals   People who do bad things, people who break the law.

Devil   An angel who was sent away from heaven. God's enemy.

Doubting   When you're not sure if something is true.

False   Something that is not true.

Forgive   When you forgive someone who has hurt you, you're not cross with them any more.

Holy Spirit   The Spirit or Holy Spirit is a person. He is God at work on the earth.

Jewish   Belonging to the religion of the Jews. Jews believe in the God of the Old Testament. They do not believe that Jesus is the Son of God.

Offerings   Like presents that people give to God.

Passover   An important Jewish holy day when the people had a special meal to remember how God set them free.

Praise   To tell God (or a person) how good they are.

Priests   People who lead the services in a church or synagogue.

Prophets   People who listen to God and then tell people what he has to say.

Scriptures   The Bible, also called the Word of God.

Synagogue   A Jewish church.

Temple   A big church where people went to worship God.

Tomb   A place where dead bodies are put, like a grave.

Notes for carers and helpers

These Bible guides are designed to help a wide range of people who need extra help. It's impossible to tailor Bible notes to fit everyone's needs. But our hope is that many who have some level of visual or intellectual disability or just need a simpler approach can be helped to pray and read the Bible regularly through this series.

Some people will be able to use these notes without any help from others. But if you are the carer or helper of someone needing some assistance with using them, here are a few pointers which may be useful to you.

Before you begin, ask the Holy Spirit to help communicate the main thought from each reading and note to the person you are reading with. God through the Holy Spirit can communicate on levels that we cannot! Part of the Holy Spirit's role is to make Jesus real to people and you are working in partnership with him.

Make sure you have the person's full attention before starting to read. Think about how you can eliminate auditory or visual distractions in the environment such as TV or other people's conversations. Try to find a quiet place. Use eye contact to maintain good connection.

Read slowly and clearly, pausing where suitable. Facial expressions, hand and body movements can all help to underline the meaning of the material. Encourage whatever response is appropriate, particularly in prayer and praise.

Use your knowledge of the person to assess how much is being understood, how much clarification might be needed and how best to make applications more relevant.

Make your time together an opportunity for learning and fellowship for both of you.

Other titles in the Bible Prospects series:

Being like Jesus

God gives new life

In the beginning

Moses, man of God

Songs of praise

The first Christians

The story of Christmas

Bible Prospects on audio A number of these titles are available as audio CDs by mail order from Causeway PROSPECTS PO Box 351, Reading, RG30 4XQ. Phone 0118 9516 978. Email causeway@prospects.org.uk

Scripture Union produces a wide range of Bible reading notes for people of all ages and Bible-based material for small groups. SU publications are available from Christian bookshops. For information and to request free samples and a free catalogue of Bible resources:

✧   phone SU's mail order line: local rate number 08450 706006

✧   email info@scriptureunion.org.uk

✧   fax 01908 856020

✧   log on to www.scriptureunion.org.uk

✧   write to SU Mail Order, PO Box 5148, Milton Keynes MLO, MK2 2YX